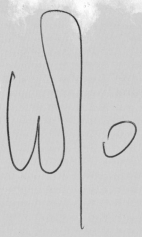

THE PARENT SWAP SHOP

FRANCESCA SIMON

Illustrated by Pete Williamson

Orion
Children's Books

First published in Great Britain in 2011
Orion Children's Books
An imprint of Hachette Children's Group
Part of Hodder & Stoughton
Carmelite House
50 Victoria Embankment
London EC4Y 0DZ

5 7 9 10 8 6

Text © Francesca Simon 2011
Illustrations © Pete Williamson 2011

ISBN 978 1 4440 0267 6

A catalogue record for this book is available from the British Library.

Printed and bound
in China

An Hachette UK Company
www.orionchildrensbooks.com

For the one and only Ava Rose

CHAPTER I

Ava had terrible parents.

They nagged.
"Have you done your spelling?"

They fussed.
"How did your shoes get so dirty?"

They ordered her about.

"Clean your room! Don't interrupt!

Use your fork. No more telly!
Do your homework!
Go to bed!"

Ava's parents always said they were telling her what to do for her own good. Ava didn't believe them. They just love being bossy, she thought.

She scooped up noodles with her fingers and stuffed them in her mouth.

"Ava! How many times do I have to
tell you? Use your knife and fork!"
snapped Mum.

"And chew with your mouth shut!"
snapped Dad.

NAG!
NAG!
NAG!

thought Ava.

I am sick and tired of being
bossed around.

Ava knew exactly what kind of parents she wanted.

Parents who let her eat sweets all day. Parents who never made her go to bed, or eat vegetables, or do anything she didn't want to do.

I bet I have the worst parents in the world, she thought, after Dad moaned at her about her untidy room and Mum told her off for breaking her CD player, even though it was an accident.

One day Ava was walking slowly home from school. She'd got all ten words wrong in her spelling test. Mum and Dad would not be pleased.

Who cares about spelling, anyway? she thought, scuffing her new shoes along the pavement.

Why shouldn't she spell words the
way she wanted to?

A multi-coloured card lying on the
ground caught her eye. She picked it
up and read:

THE PARENT
SWAP SHOP

TRADE IN YOUR UNSUITABLE
PARENTS FOR BETTER ONES!

COME AND FIND THE
PERFECT PARENTS!

HUGE SELECTION! SATISFACTION GUARANTEED.
IMMEDIATE COLLECTION. PHONE TODAY!

Wow. Ava could hardly believe her eyes.

This was brilliant.
This was extraordinary.
This was fabulous.

She could trade in the two grumps she lived with and get some nice parents instead.

Ava tucked the precious card safely into her coat pocket. One more nag at me, she thought, and they're swapped.

The very next day. . .

"Don't lean back in your chair!"
said Mum.

"Stop eating with your fingers!"
said Dad.

"Stop playing with your food!"
said Mum.

Then Dad moaned about her terrible
handwriting. Mum moaned about her
terrible reading. They both moaned
about her rudeness, her laziness
and her greediness.

Ava had had enough.
"That's it!" she shrieked.

"I'm taking you to the Parent Swap Shop!"

Before they could say another word
Ava's parents were wrapped, packed,
and despatched.

CHAPTER 2

The Parent Swap Shop was crammed
with parents of all shapes and sizes.

Many held signs.

"Must eat spinach every day."

"Bedtime at 6 o'clock."

"Generous pocket money!"

Ava felt very excited. Brand-new
parents! And this time, *she'd* choose.

No bossy boots. No naggers.

No vegetable eaters.

She saw her own parents sitting with the new arrivals. Their sign read:

FIRM
BUT
FAIR

Humph, thought Ava. I'm not surprised they haven't been chosen.

Ava wandered among the parents
on display.

"Do you like children?" she asked.

"Not much," sniffed the fat mum.

"Not at all," snapped the skinny dad.

"Next,"
said Ava.

"Do you have a sweet day?" she asked.

"No," said the bald dad.

That sounded good. Was every day
sweet day?

"That's because we don't allow sweets,"
said the skinny mum.

"Next,"
said Ava.

"What time is bedtime?" she asked.

"7 o'clock," said a small mum.

Ava frowned and made a note.

"Next,"
said Ava.

"Do children have to help with chores?" she asked.

"Of course," said a tired dad. "I can't do all the work myself."

"Next,"
said Ava.

Then she stopped in front of a smiling,
red-haired mum and dad.
Their sign read:

★ ★
★ **Your** ★
wish
★ **is our** ★
★
Command
★ ★

Ava looked at them. They smiled back.

"Hi there, young lady," said the dad.

"Hello," said the mum, smiling. "You look like a lovely child."

"Will you be my slaves?" asked Ava.

"Of course," said the dad. "Parents exist to serve children."

"You name it, we do it," said the mum. "It's fun, fun, fun with us!"

This was more like it!

"I'll take them!"

said Ava.

CHAPTER 3

"Let's play chequers!" said Ava.

"Then Snakes and Ladders,

then Chess, then Old Maid . . ."

"I'm too tired right now," said New Mum. "Go and fetch me a big bag of crisps."

Ava opened her mouth to protest, then shut it. She'd get the crisps and have loads too. But next time New Mum had better get them herself.

New Mum grabbed the jumbo bag, ripped it open and stuffed her face.

"Hey, leave some for me," said Ava.

"Sorry, all gone," said New Mum,
shovelling the last crisps in her mouth
and dropping the packet on the floor.

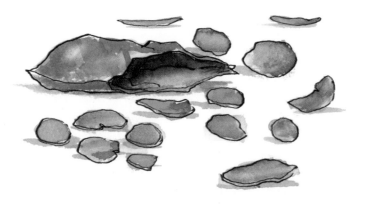

"That's not fair," said Ava.

New Mum gave her a sharp look.
"I decide what's fair," she snapped.

New Dad lit up a cigar.
"There's no smoking here,"
said Ava, coughing.
"Smoking harms children."

New Dad blew out a smoke ring and
put his feet up.

"Tough luck," he said. "I'm the boss and I'll do what I like."

"You said my wish was your command," said Ava.

"I lied," said New Dad, clicking on the TV. "Now go away and leave us alone."

Ava left the room and went
to the phone.
"Parent Swap Shop?" she said.
"I have a collection for you."

CHAPTER 4

When Ava returned to the Swap Shop most of the parents she'd seen that morning had already gone, and new ones had arrived.

So many children
making swaps, and all
thinking their parents
were the worst in the
world, she thought,

as she pushed and
shoved her way
through the crowds.

Pick 'n'
Mix

FUN!

Her parents were still there, she noticed, but had been moved to the reject section with all the other dusty leftovers.

For a moment, she felt like waving to them, but didn't. They don't deserve it, she thought. If they hadn't nagged her so much, they wouldn't be here now.

Ava moved quickly round the busy shop. She'd get it right this time.

She rejected parents who didn't give
loads of pocket money,

strict parents, parents who
set bedtimes,

and parents
who believed
in knives and
forks

and not
leaning
back at the
table.

Ava had almost been round the whole
shop when she saw a new set of
parents being unloaded.

Their sign read:

We
don't
mind
what
you
do!

Ava ran up to them.

"Do you let children eat loads of sweets?" asked Ava.

"Of course," said the dad, smiling.

"All day if you like," said the mum, smiling.

Oooh,
thought Ava.

"And when's bedtime?" she asked.

"No bedtimes in
our house,"
beamed the dad.

"Stay up all night
if you like," beamed
the mum. "We
don't mind."

Ava could hardly believe her good luck.

She glanced round to make sure no
other children were nearby.

"How often do I have to go to school?"
she asked. That was her killer question.

"Whenever you feel like it,"
said the dad.

"Whenever you're tired of playing,"
said the mum.

WOW, thought Ava,
WOW.

How could any child have traded in
these jewels?

Then Ava asked her
final question.
"What about eating
vegetables?"

"We like chocolate best
ourselves," said the mum.

"Here, have some," said
the dad, breaking off a
huge chunk.

"Woo hoo!" shrieked Ava.
"I'll take them!"

CHAPTER 5

Ava had chocolate for breakfast.

Ava had chocolate for lunch.

"Eat what you like whenever you like," said New Mum.

"Great," said Ava.

This is the life, she thought.
New Mum and Dad didn't mind
what she did, what she ate, or when
she went to bed.

No one nagged her. No one bossed her
around. No one made her wear her
coat, wash her face, or do
her homework.

For dinner, Ava had two enormous
hot fudge sundaes.

"This is heaven," said Ava, leaning back in her chair.

CRASH!

Ava fell to the floor.

"Ouch!"
yelped Ava.

But no parents ran in to check if she was all right. Ava's head hurt from her fall, but she didn't let that stop her staying up late watching TV and eating sweets.

Ava woke up on the floor at 3 o'clock in the morning with a tummy ache. Her eyes hurt from watching so much TV. Her stomach hurt from eating so much chocolate. Her teeth hurt from chomping on so many sweets.

Perhaps I'd better eat a little less
chocolate tomorrow, she thought,
clutching her aching tummy.
She dragged herself to bed and tucked
herself in as best she could.

Next day was Monday.

Ava decided to skip school. She was so
tired after her late night she fell asleep
on her beans on toast (she'd decided
against chocolate for lunch).

New Mum and Dad didn't tell her off.

In fact, they didn't bother with her much at all, other than to smile and agree to whatever she asked.

"Having fun, dear?" asked New Mum.

Actually, she was bored and lonely. To tell the truth…

"Enjoy yourself," said New Dad.

"Wait," said Ava.
"Can I play with matches?" she asked.

"Sure," said New Dad.

"Can I dance on the roof?"

"Go ahead," said New Mum.

These parents were unbelievable.
"But . . . " said Ava. "Aren't you
worried I'll hurt myself?"

"No," said New Mum,
smiling. "If you fall,
you fall."

Her real parents had nagged too much,
thought Ava. On the other hand,
they had cared about her.
These parents didn't care what she did,
good or bad.

Perhaps it was time for a swap.

CHAPTER 6

"Mum! Dad!" shouted Ava, racing through the Parent Swap Shop. "I've come to take you back!"

HUGS

SWEETS!!
PIZZA!

She stopped in the reject section.

"Mum? Dad?"

She looked around wildly.

Her parents were gone.

Ava ran to the check-out.

"Who's got my parents?" she asked.

The assistant looked them up in a large book.

"Gone yesterday," he said. "Hard to shift, those two. Never mind, just choose some others. There are plenty here."

"I don't want any others," said Ava.
"I want them."

"Sorry," said the assistant.

Suddenly there was an ear-splitting
scream as a delivery came
through the door.

A red-faced girl marched in, kicking
two unhappy-looking parents.

They looked like . . .

they were . . .

Ava's!

"Goodbye and good riddance!"
shouted the girl.
"I'm glad you're not my real parents.
Mummy! Daddy!" she cried, dashing
up to the parents Ava had brought in.

"I'm so glad I
found you! I
made a terrible
mistake! They
were so mean,
they wouldn't
let me stay up
all night..."

Slowly Ava
walked
over to her
parents.

They did not seem to notice her.

"What a horrible girl," said Mum,
rubbing her ankle. "So spoiled, so
ungrateful, so demanding. When I
think about our dear Ava..."

"I think we may have been a little hard
on her," said Dad.

"Too critical," said Mum.

 "Too bossy," said Dad.

"When was the last time we said 'well done'?" said Mum.

"I can't remember," said Dad.

They looked sadly at one another.

Then Mum saw her.

"Ava!" said Mum.

"Ava!" said Dad.

"We've missed you," said Mum.

"Humph," said Ava.

"Ava, won't you give us another chance?" said Mum.

"What about all that nagging?" asked Ava, not looking at them.

Ava's parents glanced at one another.
"We'll try to be better," said Dad.

There was a long silence.

"Okay," said Ava grumpily.
But inside she was smiling.

Of course things weren't perfect.
Dad still nagged Ava about spelling.
Mum still nagged about leaning back in
her chair. But they said nice things too.
And Ava still has the Parent Swap Shop
phone number tucked away in
her secret drawer.

Just in case.